DAV

Y Horn
984
CRA The Crane

Lilly Library
19 Meadow St
Florence, MA 01062
584-0331

Mar 1989

THE CRANE

BY
GABRIEL HORN

EDITED BY
JUDY LOCKWOOD

PUBLISHED BY
CRESTWOOD HOUSE
Mankato, MN, U.S.A.

LIBRARY OF CONGRESS CATALOGING IN PUBLICATION DATA

Horn, Gabe.
  The crane

  (Wildlife, habits & habitat)
  Includes index.
  SUMMARY: Describes the physical characteristics, behavior, lifestyle and natural environment of various species of cranes, with an emphasis on the whooping crane and sandhill crane.
  1. Whooping crane—Juvenile literature. 2. Sandhill crane—Juvenile literature. [1. Whooping crane. 2. Sandhill crane. 3. Cranes (Birds)] I. Lockwood, Judy. II. Titles. III. Series.
  QL696.G84H67   1988   598'.31—dc19   88-12031
  ISBN 0-89686-393-X

International Standard **Book Number:** 0-89686-393-X	**Library of Congress** **Catalog Card Number:** 88-12031

PHOTO CREDITS:

Cover: DRK Photo: Jeff Foott
DRK Photo: (Gary R. Zahm) 16, 32; (David Smart) 22; (Jeff Foott) 24-25; (Stanley Breeden) 34-35; (Belinda Wright) 37; (Tom A. Schneider) 28
Tom Stack & Associates: (W. Perry Conway) 4; (Jeff Foott) 6, 10, 13, 27, 41; (Wendy Shattil) 9, 15, 19, 21; (John Cancalosi) 20; (G. C. Kelley) 30-31; (Brian Parker) 39

Produced by Carnival Enterprises.

CRESTWOOD HOUSE

Box 3427, Mankato, MN, U.S.A. 56002

TABLE OF CONTENTS

Cranes live on six of the seven continents.

INTRODUCTION:

In our world there are presently 15 recorded species of the family *Gruidae*, which are most commonly called cranes. Ranging over six of the seven continents, they could be called the oldest birds in the world. Fossils of cranes date back to the Eocene period, some 40 million years ago. Bones of a bird related to today's Sandhill crane have been discovered in Nebraska, and date back four million years. The North American Whooping crane has been soaring over this vast continent for at least 500,000 years!

Today, many species of cranes are found all over the world. This book will concentrate on cranes of North America: the Whooping crane and the Sandhill crane.

CHAPTER ONE:

A century ago, North American Whooping cranes numbered in the thousands. Today, however, Whooping cranes are one of the rarest birds on earth. In 1941, naturalists estimated that only 19 to 24 of these cranes were living. On the verge of extinction, they now represent all the endangered and threatened wildlife of our time.

Today, Whooping cranes are one of the rarest birds on earth.

An incredible bird

Try stretching out your arms the length of a bed: that's about the length of a Whooping crane's wide, white, black-tipped wings. With closed eyes, picture silently riding the air currents above the billowy clouds: that's how high a Whooping crane flies.

The whooper's wingspan is more than seven feet (2 meters) long. It can fly faster than 40 miles (64 kilometers) an hour. That's as fast as a cross-country train. The whooper's magnificent wings can carry it more than 14,000 feet (4,267 m) high.

Imagine standing face to face with a Whooping crane on the ground. Whooping cranes stand five feet (1.5 m) tall. They are the tallest birds in North America, and some of the tallest birds in the world!

The head and face of the Whooping crane are covered with red skin, sparsely accented with fine, black feathers. The crane's eyes have dark pupils set in a yellow iris. Though it may not see as well as an eagle, hawk, or other bird of prey, a crane has far better vision than a human. As a wading bird, a crane can spear a crab or forage for insects and worms with its yellow beak. With the exception of the black-tipped wings, the feathery body of the whooper is all white. It stands tall and proud on long black legs.

The dance of the Whooping crane

When they are five or six years of age, the mature Whooping cranes seek mates. Mate selection can begin when the birds are as young as two years old. Whoopers select mates by mutual attraction. Two males won't compete for one female.

When the male and female whooper are ready to mate, the plumes begin to show — and how they show!

These magnificent plumes are the cranes' decorative feathers. One of the only times that the sex differences between male and female cranes is obvious is during courtship. A trained and watchful human eye will notice the more aggressive male. The male often is the first to perform the ritual of the courtship dance. The sounds or "trumpeting" calls created by both male and female at this time are synchronized so closely that the calls may sound as if they come from one bird. This dancing and trumpeting ritual is famous throughout the world.

With long, white plumes adorning a lean and powerful frame, the male bows to the female. If she responds, the two will begin a series of graceful movements and synchronized sounds that are a wonder to see and hear. Sometimes the dance will be brief, lasting only minutes. Other times the dance lasts longer. The two whoopers sway and swing sideways. They bow and bound, leaping six to eight feet (1.8 to 2.4 m) straight up on those long, black legs. Seldom, if ever, will their eyes meet during this ritual. To do so could be considered an offensive and threatening act.

The dance of the cranes with its bows and bounds may seem awkward; the sounds they make may seem loud. But many people describe the cranes' courtship ritual as a bird's ballet of grace and beauty. In this ritual of dance, the Whooping cranes seem to celebrate life and the ways of nature. Their loud trumpeting, "Ker-looo, ker-lee-

Once they've chosen each other as mates, two whoopers will spend the rest of their lives together.

oooo! Ker-looo, ker-lee-oooo!" declares their place in the world.

Once the courtship is complete and the mating dances have established two birds as a pair, the Whooping cranes will spend the rest of their lives together. In the wild, this could last 20 to 30 years! Should one of the pair die, the surviving whooper will not select another mate. It is no wonder the Whooping crane and its Sandhill crane cousin are regarded by many people as symbols of love and faithfulness.

Nesting, a shared responsibility

In the northeastern tip of the Canadian province of Alberta, and extending into the vast Northwest Territory, is an isolated area known as Wood Buffalo National Park.

It is a sanctuary for the last remaining wild buffalo in North America, as well as the sole breeding grounds of the North American Whooping crane.

Whoopers chose a nesting site that is hidden by cattail stalks or other tall plants.

Whooping cranes need space and privacy. These elusive and secretive birds can find their privacy on the clear and shallow lakes of Wood Buffalo National Park. Hidden in the swamp grass behind clustered cattail stalks, or any protective plants ranging from two to four feet (0.6 to 1.2 m), the male and female build their nest. Sometimes one of the birds rearranges a "mattress" of old brown sedge from the two-foot (0.6-m) deep water. Old sedge resembles grass except it has a solid, rather than hollow, stem and is easy to bend. This provides a sturdy and workable nesting material.

When the cranes' new home is complete, it's about three feet (0.9 m) across, and stands about one foot (0.3 m) higher than the water's surface. This elevation keeps the nest dry. The nest's location makes it possible for the cranes to see above the tall reeds in any direction. This helps keep the nest safe from most predators. Though they return to claim their same territory at Wood Buffalo National Park every spring, the Whooping cranes build a new nest each time they return.

Not long after the nest is built, the female lays her first egg. It is usually a dull, olive-green color, speckled with brown. The egg is only four inches (10 centimeters) long. A couple of days later, the female lays another egg. Both the male and female take turns nestling the new egg beneath their soft breasts. Carefully, each will gently turn the eggs with his or her beak. This helps the embryos (the undeveloped birds inside the eggs) develop properly. It is during this time that the Whooping crane receives its reputation as a fearless defender and protector. The whooper uses its yellow beak as a deadly spear against predators. Its loud trumpeting alarm can even frighten away bears!

The newborn

Slight movements within the first egg can be felt by the parents about 31 days after the egg is laid. The new chick can take a whole day to chip and peck its way out of the shell. A tiny egg tooth, a small protrusion extending from its beak, helps the chick break through the shell. When the egg finally breaks open, the young crane immediately begins the cry, "Cheep, cheep. Cheeep." He's hungry!

The newborn whooper looks like a little chicken, except it's a bit larger. With long, spindly neck and legs, he appears more gawky than barnyard chicks. The chick is covered with soft, fluffy down on the wings, back, and breast. The down is various shades of orange.

Two days after the first egg hatches, the second egg splits in two, and there's another bedraggled little chick. Together, these two crane chicks are called a clutch.

The chicks spend their early days together eating

the softened worms or insects from their parents' beaks or playfully fighting over the same morsel. Only one chick will survive, however. The other will fall victim to the driving, icy rains of March, become ill, or fall prey to a predator. This happens even though neither parent strays more than 100 yards (91 m) from the nest.

The parents will continue to feed and care for the surviving chick. At about a month old, the two-foot (0.6-m) chick begins eating some insects and worms on his own. Having learned from his parents how to forage among the cattail stalks and sedge, he can give

A whooper's chick is full grown in only nine weeks.

13

a grasshopper a good chase. In nine weeks, he is almost full grown and finds food for himself.

A young crane born in late March takes flight for the first time in September. With the autumn approaching quickly, he must fly, and fly well! The edges of the lakes at Wood Buffalo Park become icy, and the first snow begins to fall. It is time for the Whooping cranes to migrate south. The older male might begin to dance. Perhaps it is a dance to develop the strength to fly great distances. Maybe he dances away the anxiety and restlessness before the flight. Then suddenly up, up, he circles, his mate and young one following. With necks and legs stretched straight out, they flap their wings. Rising high above the shaggy buffalo, the family of three cranes now aim their beaks south.

For the adults, the migratory route, or flyway, to their winter refuge is familiar, but the young one is not aware of the 2,500-mile (4,023-km) journey ahead. Indeed, it will be a long month, filled with many adventures and many dangers.

South for the winter

Flowing through Nebraska and the center of the North American continent is the Platte River. Shallow, wide, and murky, it remains one of the most

The whoopers migratory route is 2,500 miles long!

important rest stops for migratory birds, especially the Whooping crane. On any pale, yellow dawn in March or November, the Platte River becomes a bird haven.

When the whoopers arrive, they may dance to announce their presence, or they may simply dance for joy. Sometimes only one or two cranes participate in the dance. Sometimes the entire flock will dance!

15

Whoopers migrate to the Aransas National Wildlife Refuge in Texas.

The resting period lasts only a few days for the cranes. Once they have refreshed themselves, they take off and continue south.

During the long migratory journey, the whoopers face many natural and man-made dangers. Rain and wind storms make it difficult to fly on course. Natural predators await them at some rest stops. Farm and industrial chemicals pollute the water, and contaminate the cranes' main food supply at others. Hunters mistakenly shoot the crane because they think it is a snow goose. Some whoopers get tangled in power lines.

One of the great men to defend the Whooping cranes' migratory route was Robert Allen. Until his death in 1963, no one knew more about these magnificent birds. Allen urged the government to establish a federal refuge along the Platte River. He strongly believed that if the cranes were to survive this century, they should be guarded on their remaining migratory routes.

It would be hard for us to imagine taking a car trip across country without taking a rest. Without a place to stop and buy gasoline, visit the restroom, grab a bite to eat, or just stretch our legs and relax, the trip would be impossible to make. Cranes, too, need rest spots. Along their migratory routes, there are several lakes and rivers where cranes rest.

Robert Allen and other citizens learned about some of these "sky trail" rest stops for cranes. They helped protect some of these places, setting up state and federal wildlife refuges where a crane or any migratory bird could rest peacefully. Unfortunately, many of the cranes' protected and unprotected rest areas along their migration route are changing or are already slated for development. Others have totally disappeared. Even though federal law now protects the Whooping crane everywhere, without migratory rest areas, the birds may disappear.

The last winter refuge

The great white birds soar several thousand feet above the state of Texas. Nearing the shore of the gleaming Gulf of Mexico, they spot the tiny line of barrier islands which sprinkle the coast. Wisps of white clouds pass beneath their black-tipped wings. After their long journey, the cranes spy the island of Matagorda and the anxious whoopers descend.

Circling down, down, they glide past a busy intercoastal waterway that serves the traffic of barges carrying oil and chemicals. Finally, the Whooping cranes land in their last winter sanctuary in the world, the Aransas National Wildlife Refuge.

Thanks to the influence of several people, including newspaper cartoonist and conservationist "Ding" Darling, the federal government purchased enough land at Aransas so the migratory whoopers could reestablish their territory. For now, they are somewhat safe. While wintering here, they eat grasshoppers and probe the shallow pools. Using their beaks like spears, they strike at blue crabs, shrimp, and fish.

Here the whoopers and all endangered species are protected by law. They cannot be disturbed. But what can protect them when an oil well explodes? This is what happened in 1979. Fortunately, man-made booms helped trap the black sludge, and winds blew in the right direction. The area's natural bays, estuaries, and marshes helped prevent the oil slick from reaching the cranes' nests. Aransas and the whoopers' nests were saved.

Though the dangers of that oil spill are over, other dangers loom each day. Should a hurricane, another oil spill, or even a leak from a barge loaded with toxic chemicals threaten Aransas, it could be all over for the last of the wild and free Whooping cranes.

The Sandhill crane (left) is about one foot shorter than the Whooping crane (right).

The Sandhill crane displays a red cap and grey feathers.

CHAPTER TWO:

The Sandhill cranes are the oldest living birds in the world! They date from the Eocene period, over nine (and possibly 40) million years ago. Subspecies of this ancient creature, the *Grus canadensis*, have ranged from Florida to Cuba, from the Great Plains of North America to Canada, and farther into northeastern Siberia.

Silvery grey plumage covers the Sandhill's body. Its

Like the whoopers, Sandhill cranes mate for life.

short, black bill is very powerful—it can search out grain or spear insects and water creatures. Above the orange iris of the crane's eyes is its naked, red cap. Because the Sandhill's eyes are so near the top of its head, it can stretch its long neck out full length and peek above hill crests and tall plants without being seen.

The Sandhills are about one foot (0.3 m) shorter than their younger Whooping crane kin. The Sandhill is one of North America's tallest and most fearless birds.

Sandhills travel over the Rocky Mountains to their winter home.

Within the boundary of snow-capped mountains and wide rolling meadows lies the marshland of Grays Lake National Wildlife Refuge in southeastern Idaho, nesting site of the Sandhills. Like the whoopers, the Sandhills mate for life and occupy the same nest site year after year. Having built their nests in shallow water, shielded by plants, they guard their two eggs. If the eggs hatch, chances are the chicks will be foraging the marsh for soft insects by late spring.

But the parents are always close by. People and animals who venture out on the shallow banks of the lake would not get far. The Sandhill cranes come charging and trumpeting their alarms and warnings.

Migration along the flyway

Today as many as 2,000 Sandhills travel a flyway from their summer home at Grays Lake. Over the Rocky Mountains they glide on thermal currents above 14,000 feet (4,267 m) at times, at a speed of 50 miles (80 km) per hour. They have been known to cross the Continental Divide in Colorado, covering as many as 500 miles (804 km) in less than 30 hours!

Where are they headed? They're soaring south for their winter sanctuary at Bosque del Apache, a wildlife refuge in southwestern New Mexico. Here the young will mature and, like the Whooping cranes,

Bosque del Apache Wildlife Refuge in New Mexico is the Sandhill's winter sanctuary.

24

learn to live on their own.

On the 800-mile (1,287-km) trek, the Sandhill parents will encourage their young to be independent. Though they'll still allow the young one to follow them, they will ignore his cries for food.

On the flyway the Sandhill family will pass over a changing land. Sprawling cities like Denver, Colorado, have replaced scattered circles of tepees. Farms have replaced prairies and marshes.

Eager goose hunters sometimes mistake the federal- and state-protected Sandhills for geese and kill them. New Mexico now makes selected hunters pass a bird-identification course in order to hunt during goose-hunting season.

The dance of the Sandhills

The North American Whooping and Sandhill cranes are known worldwide for their particular dances. During their complicated movements and bows, Sandhills can leap 12 feet (3.6 m) into the air! During these fantastic leaps, their feathery frames and spindly legs are rigid and straight. Considering that the human high-jump record stands just above seven feet (2 m), a 12-foot jump is quite a wondrous thing.

The uncommon sounds of the Whooping cranes are shared by the Sandhills. Though their calls are

Young Sandhill chicks are carefully guarded by their parents.

The Sandhill's "clutch" is protected by surrounding cattails.

somewhat different from their cousins', the Sandhills call frequently and repeatedly, "Gar-ooo-ooo, gar-ooo-ooo-ooo." So sharp is the Sandhill's hearing and so powerful are the calls that one Sandhill can be heard long before it can be seen.

Survival in a civilized world

The Sandhill has not faced near-extinction like its Whooping crane relatives. The Sandhill can live fairly close to man and does not require privacy when nesting. The Sandhills' need for territory, therefore, is not as great. However, too much encroachment on the Sandhills and their nesting places will increase the birds' chances of becoming extinct.

Adoption of a whooper

In the mid 1970s, an attempt was made to save the North American Whooping crane. One of the whoopers' eggs was "stolen" from its nest in Wood Buffalo Park by naturalists. They transplanted the egg to a Sandhill nest at Grays Lake. The idea behind the egg stealing was to see if the Sandhills would become foster parents to the whoopers' egg. If they did, the Sandhills would raise it as their own, thus beginning

To save the whoopers from extinction, scientists transplant Whooping crane eggs to Sandhill nests.

The small Demoiselle crane is nearly extinct.

a new Whooping crane flock in the North American West.

Scientists and wildlife experts figured that one of the newly-hatched Whooping crane eggs was doomed anyway in the natural process of life, so they felt it would be a harmless way to help the whooper survive as a wild and free species.

The naturalists found that the Sandhills made terrific foster parents! Unfortunately, it has not been verified if future "adopted" whoopers will mate with each other when they mature. This would be vital for a flock of Whooping cranes to flourish. Another problem is the competition that takes place over a shrinking food supply between the new whoopers and the Sandhills who are not foster parents.

CHAPTER THREE:

Cranes have been admired throughout the world. The Japanese expressed the grace and beauty of the Japanese crane in their poetry. In the ancient legends of Japan, the crane is said to live for a thousand years. As with almost all cranes, they mate for life. In Japan the *Grus japonensis* is the greatest symbol of love.

The Chinese, too, thought of the rare Siberian white or the small and nearly extinct Demoiselle cranes as symbols of grace, beauty, and love.

To the Chinese people, the white Siberian crane is a symbol of grace, beauty, and love.

Both the Japanese and Chinese peoples have the highest regard for the great physical power of cranes. They knew that a crane whose territory is threatened becomes one of the world's fiercest fighters.

In the movie *The Karate Kid*, the young hero wins his bout despite overwhelming odds by using a most powerful karate technique called "the crane." In one of the most ancient forms of martial arts, called Tai Chi´ Chuan (pronounced tie-jee-CHOO-aan), the powerful, smooth-flowing movements of the crane are taught by the great masters.

The Sarus and Crowned crane

Protected now throughout India, and inhabiting the Asian continent south through Thailand, Laos, and Vietnam, is the Sarus crane, with its black and silver wings. The tallest crane in the world, the Sarus is a sacred bird. It is believed that a human must never kill one of a pair of Sarus cranes because the surviving bird would soon die of a broken heart. Today, exotic teapots and cups with Sarus crane designs encircling them are sold in international markets all over the world.

Along the Ivory Coast of Africa to Uganda and Nigeria, where cranes are the national birds,

The Sarus crane is found throughout India and the Asian continent.

Mandingo potters etch the magnificent Crowned crane into their pottery. On the plains of Kenya and Tanzania, the proud Masai follow their herds of livestock to the banks of ancient rivers. Here they observe the Crowned crane with its head erect and its colorfully decorated body.

Symbol of love and strength

In North America, the Native Americans highly regarded the crane. They valued the great Whooping cranes' precious plumes. Cranes were symbols of loyal mates and model parents. A Native American with a crane's name could be expected to have special attributes. The whoopers' fearless protection of their nests and territories exemplified the Native Americans' own defense of their lands.

From creation accounts of Native Americans to the naming of people and clans, to their expressions through song and dance, the "great white wings" were a strong influence on Native American culture. The following song from the Ojibwa (pronounced oh-JIB-way) people of the upper Midwest is one such expression: "In the sky/ I am walking,/ A Bird/ I accompany."

Magnificent feathers are the trademark of the Crowned crane.

38

CHAPTER FOUR:

Near the shores of Tampa Bay in Florida, Jane and Jim O'Neill have set up the Wild Bird Rehabilitation and Care Center. The Center takes care of injured birds. Nearby, one can often hear the mourning sounds of birds whose mates have died. The causes of death vary. A person drove a power boat carelessly, a fisherman hooked a water bird, panicked, and cut the line, or perhaps someone irresponsibly tried out a new gun.

Of course, there are accidents. The Blue Heron who nipped his wing on a power line, the Great Egret who was blown too far out to sea in a storm, the Sandhill who drank from sewage-contaminated water—all are examples of accidents.

Close cousins

Many times concerned people call Jane and Jim about an injured crane. Often, though, the injured bird is not a crane. Blue Herons and Great Egrets are two birds most commonly mistaken for cranes. Each have those long, slender necks and tall, spindly legs.

There are obvious differences, however. The Blue Heron is blue, and the blue, downy tuft atop his head is unmistakable. On the other hand, the Great Egret is white like the Whooping crane, but only half the

The Whooping and Sandhill cranes are protected throughout the world.

size.

The most significant difference between cranes and their relatives is seen most clearly when the birds are in flight. Only the crane flies like a spear hurled in the wind. Other great birds with elongated necks and legs do not fly fully extended.

Rescuing and treating injured birds

On any rescue where an injured bird is transported by car to the Center, the bird's mate often follows the rescuers. Even if the trip is long, somehow the mate wings its way above the car. Then, perched atop some sturdy slash pine near Jim and Jane's house, it stays, leaving only to return to the nest. By mid-morning, the mate is back atop the pine — day, after day, after day.

Sometimes the injured bird can be treated, and the pair fly away together. Other times, in the wee hours of the morning when all is still, a sound comes mournfully through the dark silence. The healthy bird is crying for its dead mate.

There are also young chicks or immature birds brought to Jane and Jim because the parents of these birds did not return to the nest. The young orphans can often be placed in a pen with an adult who has suffered an amputation and can no longer survive in the wild. These adopted parents nurture the orphans until the chicks are mature enough to be set free.

Extinction means forever

There is a kind of dying that is more final than the death of a single creature. It is the death of a whole species, known as extinction.

As few as 125 Whooping cranes live in the wild. Only 15 nests may presently exist in a natural state. At one time whoopers nested as far east as New Jersey, and throughout the Midwest's bogs and marshlands. The northern shores of the Gulf of Mexico in Louisiana was another favorite breeding ground of the Whooping cranes.

But the ever-growing human population, with its expanding cities and suburbs, pollution, and waste has changed the land. So has the introduction of foreign grains and animals. They disrupt the naturally-balanced systems that sustain great birds like the whoopers. The native animals and birds, struggling for their survival among transplanted species, become pests to protective farmers.

But perhaps one of the greatest reasons for the near extinction of the Whooping cranes in the wild is their need for space and privacy. Protected areas like Wood Buffalo National Park and Aransas National Wildlife Refuge ensure that this fascinating creature will have room to survive.

MAP:

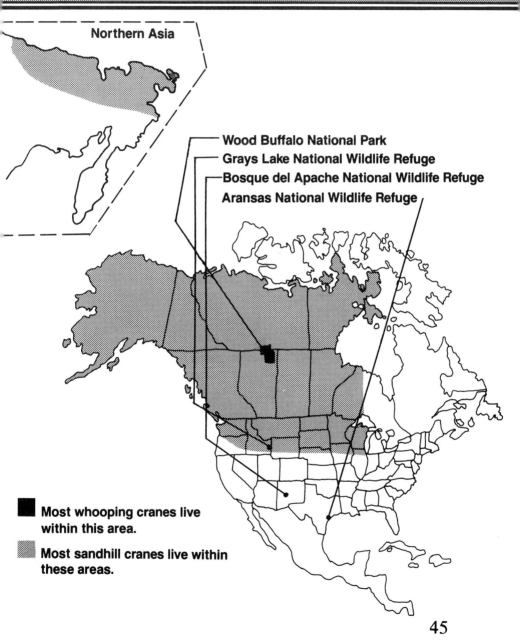

Northern Asia

Wood Buffalo National Park
Grays Lake National Wildlife Refuge
Bosque del Apache National Wildlife Refuge
Aransas National Wildlife Refuge

■ Most whooping cranes live within this area.

▦ Most sandhill cranes live within these areas.

45

INDEX/GLOSSARY:

46

INDEX/GLOSSARY:

**WOOD BUFFALO NATIONAL
  PARK** 10, 11, 14, 29, 44—*A
  protected area in the
  northeastern tip of Alberta,
  Canada. The park is the only
  remaining breeding grounds of
  the Whooping crane.*

WILDLIFE
HABITS & HABITAT

READ AND ENJOY THE SERIES:

If you would like to know more about all kinds of wildlife, you should take a look at the other books in this series.

You'll find books on bald eagles and other birds. Books on alligators and other reptiles. There are books about deer and other big-game animals. And there are books about sharks and other creatures that live in the ocean.

In all of the books you will learn that life in the wild is not easy. But you will also learn what people can do to help wildlife survive. So read on!